MISS PIGGY'S RULES

9   8   7   6   5   4   3   2   1
Digit on the right indicates the number of this printing

Library of Congress Cataloging-in-Publication Number 97-66955

ISBN 0-7624-0211-3

Cover photo by John E. Barrett
Designed by Susan Van Horn and Maria Taffera Lewis
Edited by Tara Ann McFadden

This book may be ordered by mail from the publisher.
Please include $2.50 for postage and handling.
But try your bookstore first!

Running Press Book Publishers
125 South Twenty-second Street
Philadelphia, Pennsylvania 19103-4399

MISS PIGGY'S RULES

Swine-tested Secrets for Catching Mr. Right,
Keeping Him & Throwing Him Back
When You've Had Enough

by Miss Piggy

as told to Louise Gikow and Jim Lewis

RUNNING PRESS
PHILADELPHIA · LONDON

Contents

Introduction

I'm Moi . . . and You're Not......7

Part I

Meet a Miss Piggy's Rules Girl —Moi!......9

I'm Moi . . .
and You're Not

If you were extraordinarily lucky enough to meet me, you might not think that I was particularly beautiful or charming or was more special than any other female on the planet. You would be wrong.

Actually, there is no one on the planet to compare with moi—moi's looks, charm, grace, armoire-fair.

Since no one else can be as fabulous as moi, we will have to figure out how a perfectly ordinary girl without anything especial-

ly attractive or interesting about her—you—can reach the heights of success with men that moi has achieved. Sounds hopeless, doesn't it? Well, it is. But I will do the best that I can.

Meet a Miss Piggy's Rules Girl—Moi!

Moi has always possessed a charm that is lethal to men. The world is strewn with the bodies of those who have thrown themselves off of thirty-story buildings when offered the opportunity to spend an evening in moi's company. J. C. Penny, L. L. Been, Eddy Bauer . . . the list is endless.

So who better than moi to tell you not only how to shop for a man, but how to keep him . . . and when to trade him in for a newer model?

Of course, moi has read the various books that have been published lately claiming to tell women (and men) how to succeed with the opposite sex.

I've read these books so that vous wouldn't have to . . . so that you would be able to race up to the cash registeur of your choice and shout, "Electrolux! I have found it! The solution to my problems! The anti to my dote! *Miss Piggy's Rules*! Wrap up every single copy in the store—I want to give it to my closest female friends."

On second thought . . . wrap up every copy you have in the store. Why share it with anyone?

THE FOLLOWING GUIDELINES WILL HELP TURN A SILK PURSE INTO A SOW'S EAR.

---

1. ACT NICE.
Even if you're not.

2. PUT YOUR BEST FOOT FORWARD.
The better to trip him with, my dear.

3. FOLLOW MOI'S RULES.
Remember: You can break your man,
but never, ever, ever, EVER break the rules.

That's all it takes.

This Little Piggy
Goes to Market

When you are entering le single scene, you need to think of yourself as a product. After all, you are there to sell yourself . . . complete with spiffy packaging and an aggressive marketing campaign. The important thing is, what product are you? Are you gilt-edged securities or junk bonds? Saran Wrap or expensive French perfume? Beluga caviar or dog food?

Now for the packaging (moi's favorite part). Grab those credit cards (for now, you'll have to use yours, later on, you can use his). Remember: A girl can never have too many little black dresses (or blue dresses, or red dresses, or purple dresses, or pink dresses . . .). And as moi always says: Designer, de better.

How to Look Your Best

Most of you can use a little improvement. There are plenty of books around that will tell you how to lose that unsightly cellularity by going for burnout or eating nothing but prunes. Ignore them.

The following is all you need to know:

1. DIET

There is nothing that turns a man off more than dieting. No man wants to shell out a hundred bucks for an expensive French meal only to watch his date picking at a plate of steamed brussel sprouts. Moi has always found that, as the old wive's tale goes, the way to a man's heart is through your stomach.

2. EXERCISE

Have you ever seen what a woman looks like after working out? Sweat pouring down, her face as red as a beet, her hair pointing every which way, her gym clothes a wrinkled mess. Forget it. No self-respecting male will ever be interested in vous again if he sees you looking like that. So if you must exercise, do it in the privacy of your own home.

3. WARDROBE

Many women have figure flaws, and I understand that these can be hidden by the right clothes. Unfortunately, being unflawed moi-self, I am unable to help you in this area. You're on your own.

4. COSMETIC SURGERY

There's nothing wrong with a little nipping and tucking to improve your appearance. Not that moi ever has gone under the knife. And if anyone claims otherwise—including a certain Dr. X who has been spreading rumors about moi in order to drum up patients—moi will sue.

Notice how a little Retin-A can make all the difference in your appearance.

Top 10 Places to Find Mr. Right

10. THE OFFICE

Ask for help with your computeur. Even if you're a UNIX programmer who knows her way around a 3.2-gigabyte hard drive the way other women know their way around the mall— play dumb. Men love to feel technologicalment superiour.

9. THE GYM

Remember: Wear something slinky, and don't move a muscle. You'll be the only woman who doesn't look like she just went through a car wash.

8. THE JEWELRY STORE

A perfect place to meet marriageable men. (After all, they're there to buy engagement rings, right?)

7. THE PRODUCE AISLE

Men are always trying to figure out if the cantaloupes are ripe. Stick around the fruit and vegetable section and help them out.

6. YOUR LOCAL SINGLES PLACE

All those single men behind the bar . . .

5. YOUR LOCAL LOCK-UP

All those single men behind bars . . .

4. LISTED UNDER "ELIGIBLE MEN" IN THE YELLOW PAGES

Let your fingers do the walking.

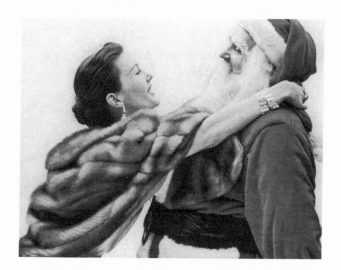

3. UNDER THE CHRISTMAS TREE

Were you a very, very good girl this year?

2. UNDER THE OBITUARIES

Read the obituaries every day for those newly single men.

1. UNDER YOUR BEST FRIEND'S NOSE

It's never too late to snatch her mate.

Personal Ads

Personal Ads can be useful in finding a male. But they use a special shorthand that can sometimes be hard to decode.

The following is a glossary of terms to help you with some of the more obscure terms so that you can perhaps locate an SM MD who is looking for VOUS.

LET YOUR ACRONYMS DO THE TALKING

SM: *Single Male*

SF: *Single Female*

SP: *Single Pig*

SF: *Single Frog*

SMURF: *Single Short Blue Person*

SMS: *Single Male Stockbroker*

SNL: *Saturday Night Live*

SOS: *Get me out of here*

DM: *Divorced Male*

DF: *Divorced Female*

DDS: *Divorced Dental Surgeon*

MD: *Male Doctor*

MUD: *Male Ugly Doctor*

DUD: *Divorced Unemployed Doctor*

DULL: *Divorced Unemployed Lonely Lawyer*

DOOFUS: *Divorced Overweight Over-ugly Financially Underwhelming Single*

Writing Your Personal Ad

Moi has only one word of advice: lie. Everyone else does. Moi once answered an ad for a tall, handsome actor who loved fine dining and the rural life. He turned out to be Porky Pig. (Now you know how he acquired that speech impediment. . . .)

A Successful Ad:

hiking to fi
you need t

evenings
fireplace
ing for me

Gorgeous, trim, blond, highly successful, extremely intelligent, and amazingly
modest SP looking for SF with Ph.D.
in L.O.V.E. with MG, CDs and lots of
shares of IBM. Send photo of MG.

If you are
am tall and
look like r

hampagne
eign travel

Outgoing, fit, SF likes walks on the beach,

An Unsuccessful Ad:

beautiful
fun, smart
r no games
to meet you

Slightly overweight, bleached blond
desperate SP looking for an SF. Any SF.
Call 555-2433.

Attractive
ISO hunk

We met on the subway last month—you

Active, inte
mother of

You've Got Male!

Technologie, moi must admit, is not moi's cup of java. But it turns out that the Internet is one big singles bar. Here are a few shorthand thingies that computer types use to communicate:

MOI'S GUIDE TO CYBER-FLIRTING'

; >)	Wink	: >O	And five Maseratis too??
: >)	Smile	:⇧l	Sure, wooden-nose.
))	Yawn	: >O	And a villa in Rome, and one in the south of France, and a 100-foot yacht???
;>J	Leer	:⇧l	Liar, liar, pants on fire!
:©)	Moi	: > o	And you want to go out this Saturday night?
8Ω)	Mr. Magoo	: !)	Okay. Pick me up at eight.
: >o	You have how much money??		
: >O	You have HOW much money??		
:⇧l	I don't believe you.		

What He's Wearing, and What It Says About What He's Thinking About You

▶ *"Mmmmm. I'd like to check out her assets."*

◀ *"Mmmmm. Wonder why she's looking at me as if I were something the cat coughed up?"*

▲ *"Mmmmm. Wonder if I should tell her about my girlfriend in Paris."*

◀ *"Mmmmm. Wonder where she got that great left hook?"*

▲ *"Mmmmm. Wonder where she got that yummy outfit?"*

◀ *"Do you have any cash? I left my wallet at home."*

"Hmmm. I'd like to take
this fabulous babe
out on the town."

"I can't wait to get you
home to meet Mother."

"I believe in big church weddings."

Who Asks Who Out?

(Or Is That "Whom"?)

O ne book says he always has to ask you out, or the relationship is doomed to failure. Another says you should be the one to do the asking. Moi says, "As long as he's paying, who cares?"

Just make sure he's ready to fork out for the fettuccine. What's so great about going Dutch, anyway? After all, the Dutch come from a small, flat country where the people wear uncomfortable foot-wear and there are a lot of dikes.

Need moi say more?

TEN SURE-FIRE OPENING LINES

1. What's your name?

2. What do you do?

3. What are you lookin' at?

4. Haven't you seen me somewhere before?

5. Where have you been, under a rock?

6. What's your sign?

7. What's your number?

8. What's your net worth?

9. What's your problem?

10. Are you going to come quietly, or do I have to get rough?

I've Got Your Number

(Or, I Know Who You Are. I Know Where You Live)

Never give a man your phone number and then wait at home for him to call.

Moi has given out moi's number countless times, and when moi tracked down the men afterwards (with the help of a nice detective agency), they all told me they had turned their apartments upside-down searching for it (which is why their apartments look the way they do, I suppose).

So unless there's a tattoo parlor next door, make sure you get his number, address, driver's license, and name of next of kin.

The Telephone

Before the telephone was invented, people had to actually get dressed and go outside to buy food. But did you know that the telephone is also your best friend in your quest to find Monsieur Right? Think of it. The phone book is simply filled with single men. All you have to do is start dialing. But what do you say to them? The following sample phone call should help.

Ring, ring, ring.

He: *Hello?*

You: Hi. I'm calling from the Publisher's Cleaning-house Sweepstakes to tell you that you are the lucky winner of ten million dollars! You just have to answer the following questions correctly to win.

He: *Omigod! Okay, okay. I'm ready!*

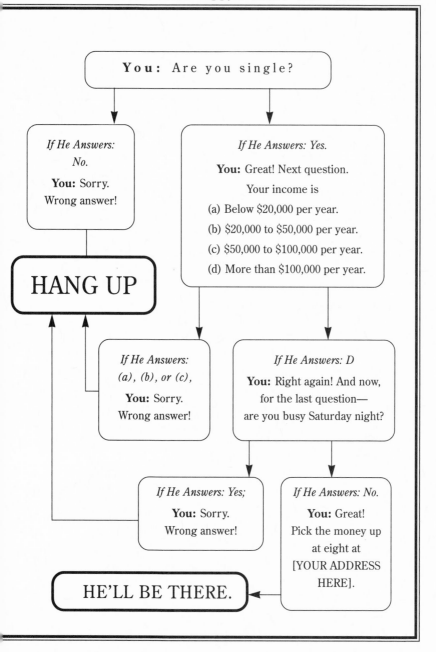

The Vous-to-Moi Quiz

Here's a quiz to help you figure out how you're doing.

YOUR P-QUOTIENT

1. He calls to tell you he's still hung up on his old girlfriend. You

☐ a. say good-bye politely and hang up.

☐ b. take him to the cleaners and hang him out to dry.

2. If you're in the mood for a romantic night out and he wants to stay home and watch the game, you

☐ a. break out the popcorn.

☐ b. break the TV.

3. You're at a party and another female is flirting with your boyfriend. You

☐ a. get him a glass of punch.

☐ b. punch him in the glasses.

4. You play hard to get by

☐ a. saying as little as possible and and acting mysterious.

☐ b. speaking softly and carrying a big stick.

5. *He puts his overcoat on to go to the men's room. You*

☐ a. spray on some Ambush and wait for him at the table.

☐ b. ambush him at the exit.

6. *A man tells you that this is your last date. You*

☐ a. smile sweetly at him and take his arm.

☐ b. smile sweetly at him and break his arm.

If you've answered (b) to all of the above questions, you are well on your way to becoming moi. If you answered (a), resign yourself to a life of solitude and misery.

The First Date

A h, getting ready for your First Date. Moi remembers it well. The excitement, the anticipation, the checklist.

The Night The magique night has arriven. You are ready and awaiting your Prince Charming. How can you ensure that this evening will be a smashing success, and that he will shout "Encore!" at the end of it? Do what les professionals do: Rehearse, rehearse, rehearse. After all, you wouldn't go on stage without knowing your lines, would you? And this could be the most important performance of your life.

First of all, do your research. After all, you want to understand his motivation! (You know yours.) Interview his friends and family. Observe him at his workplace (don't let him catch you, of course). Get to know the real he.

Now, write down everything he might say and you might reply. Practice your lines in the mirror. Bat your eyelashes. Give it all you got.

Work on your part until you can recite it backwards and forwards. If things don't go well, as they say in the theater, break a leg! (His, of course.)

DON'T FORGET TO:

1. **Bathe** *(behind the ears, too!)*.
2. **Defoliate thoroughly.**
3. **Brush your teeth.**
4. **Put on your makeup.** *Plaster of Paris makes a good foundation if you're suffering from any little blemishes. Just trowel it on and let it dry.*
5. **Dress in something low-cut and alluring.** *(If low-cut doesn't work, try your uppercut.)*
6. **Wear perfume.** *Moi's favorite these days is a charming little scent called Eau D'or.*

EAU D'OR

·PARIS·
KENTUCKY

16
fl. oz.

The Second Date

Congratulations! You made it past opening night. You're on your way to a long-running hit! How can you ensure great reviews and a booming box office? Do what the producers do. Paper the house!

- *Make sure Mother calls when your intended picks you up. Call her Tom or Brad. Tell her you can't talk but call back later.*
- *Fill the house with roses and romantic cards so that your date is sure to notice.*
- *Have your mother call again.*

When he sees that you're this much in demand, your man will hunger for more! And ask you out on . . .

The Third Date

(Or, Oscar Night!)

Congratulations! You've reached date number three! Tonight is awards night—the night when you collect. Vous have studied your lines, batted your lashes, interviewed, and bathed your way to your ultimate goal. Bravo for vous! All that hard work is about to pay off. And the award goes to—VOUS!

From now on, you are a couple. An item—C-O-M-M-I-T-T-E-D. In a relationship! You have earned the right to call yourself "girlfriend." From here on, it's only a hop, skip, and a little blackmail away to "fiancée."

When you accept the token of his esteem that accompanies this momentous occasion (be it silver, gold, or cubic zirconia), be gracious. Don't whip out your jeweler's loupe and examine the goods. (That comes later.) Say thank you, try to blush; a few tears wouldn't be out of order.

And if by some chance your date doesn't realize what night this is, remember what moi taught you back before Date One: Break a leg!

HIS WALLET AND WHAT IT SAYS ABOUT WHAT HE'S THINKING OF SPENDING ON YOU

Show Moi Le Money! Now that vous—and better yet, he—have committed, it is *très important* that vous know where the money is coming from. His wallet, of course. The wallet should be chock full of cash and credit cards for vous to use. If you cannot find enough places to spend his money, vous need to think harder.

Not enough.   **Enough.**

How'm I Doing?

A good first date:

He takes you out to dinner at that fancy new French restaurant downtown.

A bad first date:

You get the Happy Meal in the drive-thru line at that little Scottish place.

A good second date:

He brings a dozen roses.

A bad second date:

He brings a camera and wants to shoot a dozen poses.

A good third date:

He takes you home to meet his mother.

A bad third date:

He stays home. He sends his mother instead.

What He Says vs.
What He Really Means

He says:	He means:
My name is John Doe.	My name is John Doe.
I am not interested in going out with you.	I'm dying to go out with you. I thought you'd never ask!
Kiss you? Are you a fool?	Kiss me, you fool!
Leave me alone or I'm calling the police!	Leave with me right now. I'm calling the Justice of the Peace!

What You Say vs. What You Really Mean

You say:	You mean:
Haven't I seen you somewhere before?	I know who you are. I know where you live.
Saturday night? I'll have to check.	YES! YES! YES!
I don't care where we go, as long as we're together.	Whaddaya mean, we're going to MacDonald's?
Oh, what an absolutely charming restaurant!	That's better.
Isn't that a lovely diamond ring?	Buy me that diamond ring.
Uh . . . marry you? I'll have to think about it.	YES! YES! YES! YES! YES! YES! YES! YES! YES! YIPPEEEEE!!!!!!!

Questions from Some Rules-to-Be Girls

You should know all of this by now. But let's face it—some of you weren't dealt a full deck. So here are some answers to those of you in the peanut-brain gallery.

Dear Miss Piggy:
I've been divorced, and after years out of the "dating game," I'm afraid that the rules have changed.

—New to Dating

Dear New:
Don't worry. The rules are the same: No kicking, biting, or gouging. Otherwise, anything goes.

Dear Miss Piggy:
I met the most wonderful guy. On our first date, he took me to dinner and dancing and we had a marvelous time. Then he bought me a gorgeous 22-carat gold bracelet and matching earrings with diamonds and rubies in them! After that, he surprised me with a trip to the Bahamas on his private yacht! Do you think he's serious?

—In Love

Dear In:
I'd be happy to find out for you. What's his number?

Dear Miss Piggy:
I just met the man of my dreams. He's the one, I just know it!
But he has a steady girlfriend. What do I do?

—Hopelessly Devoted

Dear Hopelessly:
Call 555-4958 and ask for the Terminator.

Dear Miss Piggy:
I finally had it with my boyfriend, and I took
your advice about breaking a leg. He pressed
charges, and right now, I'm living under an
assumed name in another state.
What can I do?

—On the Lam

Dear On:
Lucky for us, we live in a
democracy. No matter what
you've done, you have the
right to an attorney. So go
out and find one: preferably,
one who's cute, single, successful,
and drives a Beemer.

The Relationship

Vous have just completed Part I of *Miss Piggy's Rules.* By now you have met—and won the eternal love of—the man of your dreams.

Some might ask: "Miss Piggy, now that I have him, what do I do with him?" But moi prefers to look at the situation this way: "Now that you have him, what can he do for you?"

Vous should always enter into any relationship seriously, as if it could be the one, true love of your life. Take stock of what he has to offer. (Also take cash, bonds, and all negotiable securities.)

Remember: great relationships are built on a foundation of mutual trust . . . and mutual funds.

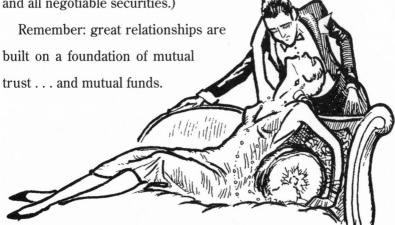

Got to Get You into His Life!

The most difficult part of becoming a couple is finding enough closet space for your stuff and finding enough trash bags for his stuff.

The following list of questions will help you tell if the time is right for taking over Mr. Right's place:

- ☐ **Do you love him? This includes everything between "like" and "lust."**

- ☐ **Does he love you? This includes everything short of a severe allergic reaction.**

- ☐ **Does he have a nicer place than you? Size matters!**

- ☐ **Is he available? Never commit to someone who is living with someone else . . . especially if it's his mother.**

- ☐ **Are you available? You've got to be kidding.**

- ☐ **Do you believe this relationship has a future? Never get involved unless you believe that your relationship is going somewhere, like St. Bart's or the south of France.**

- ☐ **In the unlikely event of a water landing, could he be used as a flotation device? It never hurts to ask.**

If you answered "yes" to one or more of the above, you're ready for commitment.

Getting Him Ready for Togetherness

Moi will never understand why men are so anxious about commitment. They believe that they will have to give up their freedom to someone who is going to tell them exactly what to do and when to do it.

To overcome men's irrational fear of commitment, vous must be very subtle. First, a few simple rules:

Rule 1. Never use the word "commitment" in his presence. For reasons that baffle medical experts, men hear this as "You're a dead man."

Rule 2. Always agree with him about everything. Don't worry. This ends the moment he commits.

Rule 3. Share his likes. If he likes to camp, break out the pup tent. If he likes football, go to a game with him—once. This not only lulls him into a false sense of security, it also gives you something to throw in his face for the rest of your lives together.

Rule 4. Share his dislikes. If he dislikes a certain person, you should dislike that person, too. Unless, of course, that person is you.

Follow these rules and you will become his heart's desire— cooperative, caring, sharing, and totally undemanding. He will be calm and relaxed around you. He will be getting sleepier. His eyelids will feel heavy.

It's time to attack.

"Now Hear This!"

Changing the way he does absolutely everything!

One moment, you are dating each other. The next, you have won the war, toppled his regime, and are living like a queen. He is indulging your every whim and feeding you those tiramisu thingies with extra powdered sugar. You are now officially a couple. There is nothing left to do but pick out a wedding ring, right?

Wrong!

You see, even the most perfect of men have their flaws. It's up to you to identify them, eliminate them, and then remake him to your liking.

There are those who say: "A man is a man is a man." And to them I respond: "What's your point, redundant-breath?" There are others who say: "Never go into a relationship thinking that you can change him." To which I counter: "True! You should always go into a relationship knowing that you can change him." After all, if you can't change him, why bother? Where's the fun? Where's the challenge? Where's the pride of ownership?

The Top 10 Things That

(. . . and what vous can do to change him)

10. He can't express his emotions.

And why can't he cry?

Solution: If you really want to see tears, force him to watch every Jane Austen movie ever made.

9. He's a bad dresser.

Solution: Make him buy a new wardrobe. (If he's a better dress-er than you, make him buy you a new wardrobe.)

8. He forgets important anniversaries.

He never gets you a gift on the anniversary of your first date.

Solution: Buy your own gift (with his credit card).

7. He's ugly and cheap, too.

Solution: Dump him.

6. He treats his dog better than he treats you.

Solution: Dump him and his dog.

5. He spends more time tinkering with the car than talking about you.

He would rather get greasy tightening a loose thingama-whatzis than have a serious conversation about how you feel.

Solution: Tell him that he had better rotate his tires in your direction or you're going to pop his clutch.

Are Wrong With Him

4. He behaves like a child.

He's just a little boy who thinks vous are his mommy and should take care of his every need.

Solution: Give him a "time out."

3. He watches sports all day.

He sits in front of the TV scarfing down chips and beer and barely notices that you're there.

Solution: This is nature's way of freeing up more time for vous to go shopping.

2. He takes your relationship for granted.

He tells you that you are the most important person in his life—and then calls you Monique.

Solution: Find out who Monique is and see that she never sets eyes— or anything else—on him again. Then cry inconsolably for two days or until he makes it up to you big time.

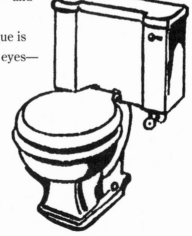

1. The "toilet seat" thing.

Solution: Super glue.

Alas, sometimes a man refuses to change. But take heart: If you can't change him, you can always exchange him. This is known in *Miss Piggy's Rules* as "trading up." Bring your loser to a place where there are lots of eligible women, tell them how absolutely perfect he is, and stand back. Meanwhile, you can choose a new man and begin again. (This might not be fair to your fellow female. But face it, sister, this sisterhood stuff only goes so far.)

Getting to Know Vous, Getting to Know Too Much About Vous

Meeting his friends and family—and surviving!

Perhaps vous are afraid of meeting people from your beloved's past. Well, get over it. Don't you want to know who he really is, how he got that way, and what he's probably going to look like in fifteen years when his hair is falling out and his teeth are sitting in a glass by the side of the bed? I know moi would.

Fasten your safety belts. It's going to be a bumpy ride!

Meeting His Friends!

Always begin by meeting his friends. Unlike his family, who he never listens to anyway—his friends will be passing judgment on vous.

There are several types of old friends. Know them, understand them, then get them out of his life as quickly as possible.

The Best Buddy.

He is the friend who will always wind up sleeping on your couch, eating all your food, and staying over the entire weekend. There's only one way to get rid of him—fix him up with someone who lives in Nome. (Unless you live in Nome, of course.)

The Sports Buddy.

It's a sunny Saturday and vous are dressed for a picnique in the park, when—ding-dong!—who is at the door but this ding-dong with his clubs in hand. The best way to lose him is to bury him in the nearest sand trap. Aiii-yaaa!

The Hunky Buddy.

He is charming, witty, and handsome. Make sure you get his phone number. Then give it to moi.

The Old Flame Who Is "Just a Friend."

Oh, spare moi! If your man expects vous to treat this hussy as a friend, then he is out of his mind. Give her a gentle hint that vous want her out. How? Well, they don't call them flame throwers for nothing.

Remember: By dumping all of his old friends, vous will be doing your man a favor. After all, it's not as if he'll have any time to be spend with them. He'll be spending his time with you.

Dealing with His Mother

Unlike friends, treat his mother as an ally. Be kind, thoughtful, and a paragon of virtuous womanhood at all times. She must think vous are too good to be true. Once you have accomplished this, she will always take your side in any argument.

The "I Know What You're Up To" Mother. This is a woman who used the same techniques you are using to land her own husband. She knows that vous are putting on an act, and she's not falling for it. There is no way to convince her that you are anything but a manipulative gold digger, since she was one herself. Write her off.

The "I Used to be a Looker" Mother. This is the mother who was once just as popular and perky as vous, and can't seem to let go of the past. Moi's advice for her: Learn to live with it, Mother!

The "Blood is Thicker Than Water" Mother.

This woman does not care whether vous are right or wrong; she will always take her son's side. The best defense against her is for vous and her son to relocate at least 3,000 miles away. Don't leave a forwarding address.

The "Let's Be Friends" Mother.

She likes you. She takes your side in every argument. She is obviously trying to get to know the real you. And once that happens, she's sure to morph into one of those other mothers. (See above.)

Don't worry. If the methods described above do not work, remember that, in the balance of power, vous hold the ultimate weapon: Someday you will decide when she gets to see the grandchildren.

"Our Little Secret!"

(Or, making him think he's still in charge)

Who's the boss? Vous are, of course! We all know this, but please, please . . . let's keep it our little secret. There is nothing worse than a whiny man with a bruised ego trying to act like he's in charge.

How do you make it look like he is in charge when you're the one doing all the charging?

Actually, there are two ways:

1. Outright dishonesty. Chortle, snicker, and guffaw at the absolute ridiculosity of such an idea! Try something like this: "Moi! In charge!? Oh, mon amour, nothing could be further from the truth! It is vous who are our guiding light! Vous who decide where we are going for dinner tonight. How about the expensive French place next to that delightful all-night jewelry store?"

2. Cushioning the truth. Break your relationship into four areas: **Money, Shopping, Working**, and **Watching TV.**

The Four Elements of Love

Subject		What you say
Money		I don't understand money. I'll let you handle it.
Shopping		I don't want to go shopping . . . unless you do.
Work		Tell me what you did at work today.
Television		We can watch whatever you want.

By saying what you mean but meaning something other than what you say, you remain the boss, he continues to think that he's the boss, and everyone is happy! And if your relationship doesn't work out, you can always fall back on a career in politics.

What he hears	What you mean	What you get
She thinks I'm a smart guy who can handle high finance.	I don't want to count it; I just want to spend it.	His money.
I'll do whatever you want.	We're going shopping.	Whatever's for sale.
She's interested in me.	While you're yammering away, I can be thinking about important things like what to order for dessert.	Dessert.
We can watch the Super Bowl!	We can watch whatever you want . . . as long as it's *The Way We Were*.	To watch *The Way We Were*.

Basic Training for Your Man

As a woman, vous have always been ready to walk down the aisle. You are the perfect bride. Now all you need is the perfect groom.

But alas! Perfect grooms are not born: they must be made. A man must be trained to lose his bad old channel-flipping, sock-tossing, sports-watching, toilet seat-up habits, and become someone who is truly worthy.

Inspired by the U.S. Marines (who, like moi, are also looking for a few good men), I have created "Miss Piggy's Boot Camp" for turning your man into an officer and a gentleman.

REVEILLE

Your man needs a wake-up call. A bugle works, but so does a bucket of ice cold water. At the first

sound of this reveille, he must be trained to leap out of bed, make the bed, and go out and earn money.

"I Can't Hear You!"

Men simply do not listen. (How many times have you delivered a brilliant monologue about the latest royal family scandal only to have him respond, "Huh?") And when they do listen, they do not hear what you really mean.

Solution: Use a large megaphone and scream directly into his ear. (It works for the Marines . . .)

Enlisted men simply do not appreciate the finer points of domestic living. They are thrown by the concept of throw pillows and constantly forget that the guest towels in the guest bathroom are there for *decorative purposes only!*

Your man must understand that the monograms on those guest towels always facing outward is essential to your well-being and happiness; that paisley pillows never go on a plaid couch; and that a plaid couch never goes in your house.

War Stories

Because men tell the same boring old stories over and over and over again, follow Josephine's lead. Whenever Napoleon started yammering on about this or that silly campaign, she would say, "Tell them the one about Waterloo where Wellington beat you," or "What's that joke you love? You know, the one about Pinocchio?" His story ruined, Napoleon would shut up, allowing Josephine to eat her napoleons in peace. It worked for her, and it'll work for vous.

Dishonorable Discharges

Men slouch, scratch, clear their throats (and blow their noses) loudly, and act like, well, men.

This one is easy. Whenever he does any of the above, just give him a swift kick. (Now you know why they call it Boot Camp.)

Latrine Duty

Quelle surprise! He leaves the seat up.

Two words: Super glue.

Telling Him About Your Future Together

Your future together holds such promise! Why ruin it by telling him your plans? Moi recommends that vous tell him you believe in living one day at a time. Meanwhile begin planning for the wedding.

The Future! Ahh, just think of it! You and your love together forever! Romance! Adventure! Commitment! Childbirth! Children! Day-care! Pre-school! What do you mean the baby-sitter can't make it? You spilled what on my new dress!? After-school music, dance, and gymnastics les-sons! Soccer practice! Little League games! Driving everyone everywhere in the minivan! What time are you going to be home for dinner? Take-out pizza . . . again!? It's going to cost how much to send them to college? No daughter of mine is going out with a thug named Slasher! Will you turn that music down!!!!

On second thought, it is probably best if vous don't think too much about the future, either.

Keeping Love Alive

*Rekindling the flames of passion when
your romance gets soggy*

Every love affair, no matter how perfect has its less-than passionate moments.

Even storied romances of the past have had their rough spots. Cleopatra had days when she thought Antony was behaving like an asp. (This is the origin of the phrase: "Our relationship is in de-Nile.") Juliet grew weary sitting in that balcony night after night wondering wherefore art thou while Romeo was out carousing at some sports bar.

And then there are the royals, but let's not go there . . .

The fact is that even moi's romances have, upon occasion, needed a jump-start. (Just be careful not to use too much voltage, which can cause internal injuries and chronic bad hair days.)

Like nature, love has its seasons. Sometimes vous are in the spring of your relationship, when love blossoms and grows. Or perhaps it is summer, when love romps barefoot through the sunshine . . . or autumn, when love cools off and falls off trees.

This section is devoted to the winter of your relationship,

when your pipes are frozen, he can't get your furnace started, and your love is buried in a ten-foot snowdrift. Get out that shovel! Call in the plows! Heat up the hearth! Vous have worked too hard to let your love get lost in this blizzard of bad metaphors.

Start practicing "More Better Moi!"

"More Better Moi!" is a simple six-step program for relighting the spark of your romance and saving your relationship. Here's how it works:

"More Better Moi"

Six Steps to Hot Stuff

STEP 1.
Moi's Doe Eyes

Batting your eyelashes is an art that takes practice and concentration, but it works when you need to bag that big buck. A few weeks ago, I was batting moi's on a train platform and this nice, single doctor came up to moi and asked if he could take the grit out of my eye . . . but that's another story.

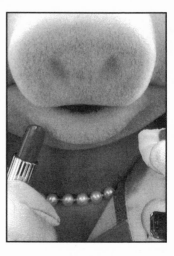

STEP 2.
Moi's Kiss-able Lips

To achieve a smoocher like moi's, drink a thick chocolate shake three times a day. Trying to get the chocolate through the straw will make your lips strong, and the ice cream will make your lips full and kiss-able.

Practice "More Better Moi" everyday for the next three months and if you don't like the results—turn to page one of this little book and start all over again.

STEP 3.
Moi's High Cheekbones

One is born with cheekbones and nothing can be done about whether they are high or low. Au contraire! For high cheekbones, do what I do: Tuck your nose down as low as it will go. This may make it difficult to breathe, but isn't true love worth the occasional blackout?

STEP 4.
Moi's Fabulous Tresses

Unlike vous, I was born with these cascading golden tresses with loads of luscious body. For the follicle-y challenged, I recommend my accessory of choice. To order, dial: 1-800-X-10-SHUNS.

STEP 5.
Moi's Luscious Figure

Some men may think they prefer bony waifs. These men are mistaken, and once you are in their weight class it is much easier to make them see the error of their ways.

STEP 6.
Moi in Motion

You've got the look, now let's get it in motion. Forget about where you're going—it doesn't matter. Just wear extremely high heels and learn to swivel those hips. Now and again you're liable to trip into a closet or fall head-over-high-heels down a mountain, but if you look good doing it, who cares?

Now of course, this "More Better Moi" program has one eensy-weensy problem: No matter how hard you try, vous can never be moi. But if this doesn't put life back into your relationship, take your man by the wrist and check for a pulse.

When Mr. Right Goes Wrong

How to tell if it's "over" and he's "out"

Men are not perfect—not even close. So we should never be surprised when they fail dismally in a relationship. Oh sure, the insensitive twits should be hung by their thumbs and covered with molasses and fire ants, but for vous and moi the time comes when we must move on to bigger and better men.

But how do vous know that the time has really come? How can you be sure that your relationship is really finished, kaput, washed up, eighty-sixed, and otherwise unlikely to last until the weekend? To help, moi has prepared this convenient quiz.

Is My Relationship Over?

1. *Are you still the first number on his speed dial?*

    ☐ Yes   ☐ No

2. *Has he gotten a pit bull and named it after you?*

    ☐ Yes   ☐ No

3. *Have you ever found another woman's fingerprints on his collar?*

    ☐ Yes   ☐ No

4. *Has he ever called you by someone else's name . . . even after you've agreed to wear a "Hello! My name is . . ." sticker?*

    ☐ Yes   ☐ No

5. *If he is seeing someone else, has he asked you to cook a dinner for the two of them?*

    ☐ Yes   ☐ No

6. *When you are shopping for an engagement ring, does he ask the salesclerk if the store has a "frequent-buyer" program?*

☐ Yes   ☐ No

7. *On your wedding day, does he ask if he can bring a date?*

☐ Yes   ☐ No

If you answered "yes" to more than one of these questions, then you had better send for more fire ants. Whichever the case, this is no time to be sad. You are now ready to learn the most important lesson in *Miss Piggy's Rules—Getting Rid of Mr. Wrong and Getting on with your Life!*

The Afterlife

Losing that Louse and Living Happily Ever After!

Miss *Piggy's Rules* are *très important* when vous are looking for love and absolutely essential when vous are in love, but they will serve vous best when—alas!—vous have lost love.

Forget him, forgive yourself, and get on with your life!

You will travel from heartache to healing, from getting even to getting even more, from losing a lover to finding the greatest love of your life—yourself.

Vous and moi are off to the land of happily ever after. Watch your step!

Breaking Up Isn't
So Hard to Do After All

By now vous have reached the decision to break up with your beau. He has broken your heart, betrayed your trust, and transgressed once too often. If there is one thing we women cannot stand it's heart-breaking, trust-betraying frequent transgressors.

But you are so paralyzed by the thought of "ending it" that you continue to go out with him until long after your love and his money are gone.

The only reason vous are afraid of "ending it" is because you think breaking up must be a painful, angry scene filled with tears and sorrow. Get over it, girl!

With *Miss Piggy's Rules*, breaking up with him is even more fun than breaking him in. Remember: Life is a party. And just because vous are getting rid of this particular dip does not mean your party is over.

One warning: It is possible to enjoy these breaking-up parties so much that you may find yourself wanting to end relationships that are still going strong. Fight the urge. Your turn will come. In the meantime, trust moi: Someone, somewhere is breaking up . . . and you're invited!

BREAK-UP PARTY IDEAS

Here's how to turn your next break-up into a festive occasion that everyone can look forward to:

Invite Friends—Your girlfriends, of course. They'll take your side, and drown out any lame rebuttal he may attempt.

Music Is a Must—Be sure to choose songs he hates—"Achy Breaky Heart" is sure to be tops on his "turn-that-off" playlist.

Make it a Catered Affair— Serve the best of everything. Just make sure he doesn't have a chance to stop payment on the check.

The Party's Over—Did someone call the cops? Wave bye-bye to Mr. America's Least Wanted as he rides off in the back of a police car. Good riddance, you louse!

Make it a Surprise—Dim the lights and have everyone hide. The element of surprise gives vous an unfair advantage.

Moi's Top 10 Reasons
You Are Better Off Without Him

*Still having second thoughts about ending
your relationship? Here are a few more reasons
why you should lose that loser.*

10. Less beer in the refrigerator means more room
for Sara Lee!

9. You no longer have to go to movies where everyone explodes.

8. You can flirt with cute guys anytime, anywhere.

7. You can reactivate the ESPN channel-blocker.

6. You can watch taped episodes of *Rosie* at dinner!

5. No more impaling yourself on his errant toenail
clippings.

4. Leftover pizza is no longer one of your major
food groups.

3. No more hair in the sink.

2. There's even more closet space for vous!

*And the number one reason vous
are better off without him . . .*

1. THAT "TOILET SEAT" THING AGAIN.

Forgetting Him and Forgiving Yourself

Forgetting him . . .

Your old relationship is over. There. That was easy! He's history! He's toast! And you are . . .

What's that vous say? You still can't stop thinking about him even though you know he was a no-account, two-timing good-for-nothing? Your mind says "good-bye" but your heart says "until we meet again."

Get a grip.

There is only one sure way to silence the yearnings of the heart: Chocolate. Trust moi, a good five-pound box of Russell Stovers will make vous forget any old flame. Oh sure, finding a new love helps too. But chocolate— chocolate is forever.

. . . Forgiving Yourself

S ome experts claim that forgiving yourself after losing love is a twelve-step process, a long and difficult journey of soul-searching and reconciliation. Face it: If you really wanted to make a long and difficult journey, you would go to the outlet mall during the holiday shopping season. I have come up with a far more convenient two-step process.

Step 1. Express your Emotions Put your pain into words. "Moi has been wounded and betrayed. That low-life slime took the delicate flower of moi's heart, pulled off the petals, and stomped it till there was not enough left to make a decent batch of potpourri. I hope his foot falls off."

Step 2. Clear your Conscience Take a moment and ask yourself: "Did I do anything whatsoever that may have in the slightest brought about this break-up?"

The correct answer to your question is: No. You did absolutely nothing wrong. Your only mistake was getting involved with that dumb slug in the first place.

Voila! You have forgotten him (who?) and forgiven yourself. You are now ready to meet the real true love of your life . . . you.

Getting on with Your Life

... And living happily ever after!

This is the moment vous and moi have been waiting for! You are almost done reading this book, and moi is almost done writing it.

By reading *Miss Piggy's Rules,* you have learned absolutely everything there is to know about love (unless of course they pay me a bundle to write a sequel.)

You were a good person when you picked up this book. You were a great person when you paid for it. And now that you have read it—and become more like moi—you are an almost perfect person.

Enjoy your own company. Celebrate your life. Remember: In a world of Mr. Wrongs, you are Ms. Right.

And on that once-in-a-lifetime day when your real Mr. Right comes along, grab him. He belongs to vous.

Of course, if he happens to be a certain short green frog, I'll tear you to pieces. That's one of moi's Rules, too.

B O N U S

Moi's Guide to Getting Even!

As moi's close, personal friend and fellow famous person,
Paul Simon, once said: "There must be fifty ways to leave your lover."
Well, believe vous moi, there are at least that many ways
of getting even with your former beau.
Here are moi's fifty favorite ways to let the former man of your dreams
know what a nightmare it was knowing him.

1. **Throw out his baseball card collection.**
   (It worked for his mother.)

2. **Fix him up with your girlfriend—the lawyer.**

3. **Hide his remote controls.**

4. **Date his boss.**

5. **Marry his father.**

6. **Get Dennis Rodman to do his hair.**

7. **Cut his TV cable on Super Bowl Sunday.**

8. **Sign him up for the record-of-the-month club.**
   (There is no way out.)

9. **Introduce him to your new biker boyfriend.**

10. **Learn to drive a big rig.** Follow him everywhere,
    side-swiping him occasionally.

11. **Contact his other ex-girlfriends and file a class action suit.**

12. **Give his car a new paint job.** Use a wire brush.

13. **Take up skywriting.** Use four-letter words.

14. **Recycle his beer can collection.**

15. **Get him a pet skunk.**

16. **Pick up his dry cleaning.** Don't return it.

17. **Get him a bumper sticker that reads "I hate cops."** Let it be a surprise.

18. **Tell the Internal Revenue Service what you really think of them.** Sign his name.

19. **Volunteer him for jury duty.**

20. **Use his CDs as coasters.**

21. **Use coasters in his CD player.**

22. **Put Limburger cheese in his heating vent.**

23. **You know his favorite pair of jeans, the ones that fit just right?**

24. **Mow his lawn to spell out the letters S-C-U-M.**

25. **Shred all of his take-out menus.**

26. **Get him a subscription to *Martha Stewart Living*.**

27. **Shred all his copies of the Victoria's Secret catalog.**

28. **Play ball with his autographed "Carl Yastrzemski" ball.**

29. **Find a worthy cause. Donate clothes. His clothes.**

30. **Videotape your favorite *Oprahs* over his collection of every *Star Trek* episode.**

31. Send angry e-mail to professional wrestlers.
    Sign his name.

32. Cut the last page out of all his unread mystery books.

33. Record a new outgoing message for his answering
    machine that includes a Surgeon General's warning
    against dating him.

34. Replace his car wax with shoe polish.

35. Replace his shoe polish with peanut butter.

36. Replace his peanut butter with Dentu-Grip.

37. Replace his Dentu-Grip with car wax.

38. Make his computer run faster by dumping everything
    out of his hard drive.

39. Run an ad for him in the "Anything Goes" section
    of the personals.

40. To help him save time, re-set all his clocks so he's
    one hour early for everything.

41. To help him save space, cut his golf clubs in half.

42. To help him save money, cancel his credit cards—
    after you've maxed them out.

43. Call his house repeatedly whenever *X-Files* is on.

44. Sell his house. Let it be a surprise.

45. Five words: "Go ahead, make moi's day."

46. Four words: "My attorney? Johnny Cochran!"

47. Three words: "My boyfriend? Fabio!"

48. Two words: "Super glue."

49. One word: "Aiiiiii-yaaaaa!!!!!"

50. Take him back.